ANT FARMERS

WENDY BYERLY   KATIE AXT

This is a farm.

This is a farmer.

2

This is an ant. This ant is a farmer, too.

females

All the farmer ants are girls.

This is mold.

Ants grow mold on their farms.
Molds grow like little plants.

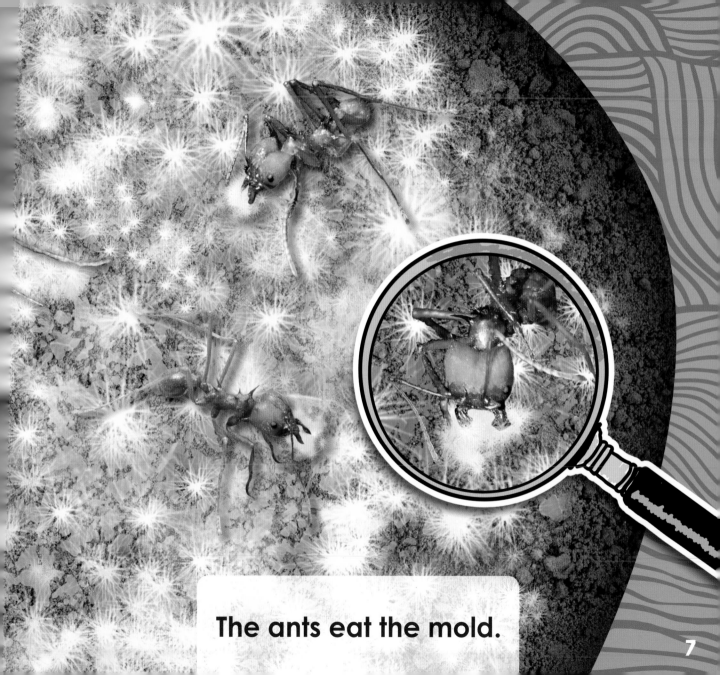

The ants eat the mold.

THIS IS HOW THE ANTS GROW MOLD.

These are leaves.

The mold eats leaves. How will the mold get leaves to eat? The ants.

First, the ants sort through the leaves to get the ones the mold likes.

Then, they lick the leaves to get off the dirt.

The ants chew up parts of the leaves into little bits.

The ants spit the leaves out here. Here it is dark. It is wet. The mold grows here.

ANT BABY

After the mold grows, the ants eat it. They feed it to their babies after they are born.

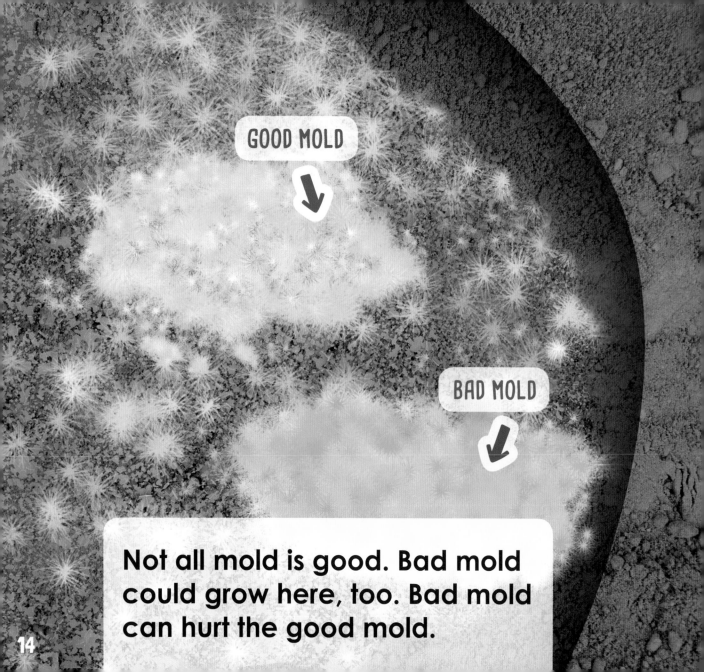

Not all mold is good. Bad mold could grow here, too. Bad mold can hurt the good mold.

The ants are smart. They can stop
the bad mold. The ants poop.

15

They stir their poop into the leaves.
Their poop helps kill the bad mold.

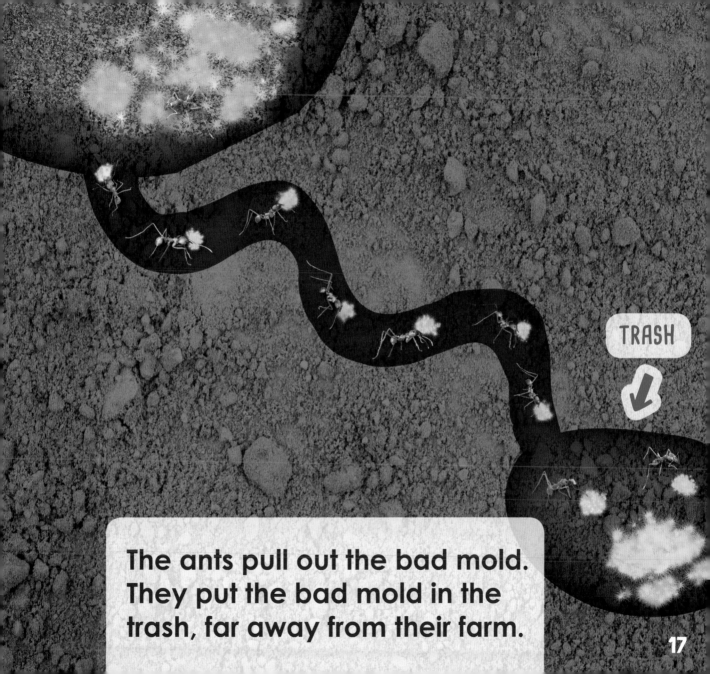

TRASH

The ants pull out the bad mold. They put the bad mold in the trash, far away from their farm.

If too much bad mold grows, the ants start a new farm.

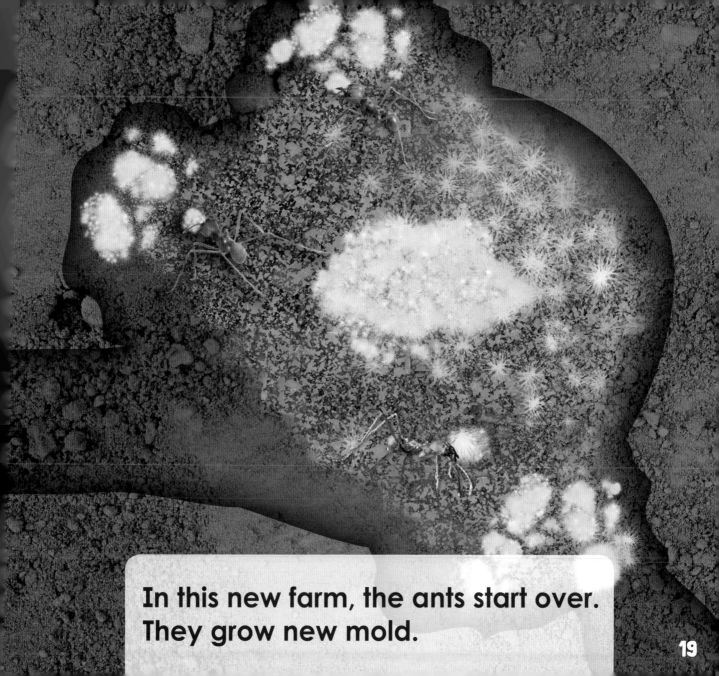

In this new farm, the ants start over. They grow new mold.

The ants can't live without the mold.
The mold can't live without the ants.
They need each other.

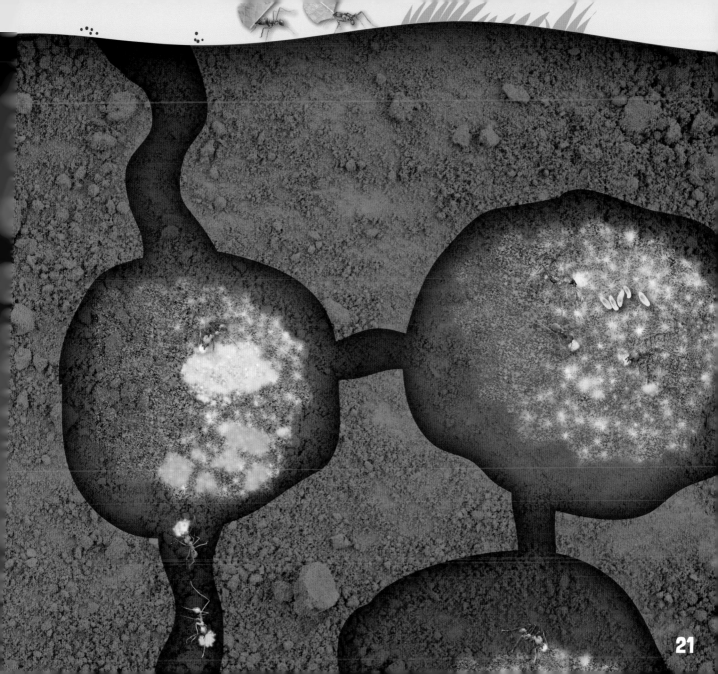

WORD ATTACK STRATEGIES

Stop	**Stop** if something doesn't look right, sound right, or make sense.
	Look at the **picture**.
s___	Say the **first letter** sound.
sp___	**Blend:** Say the first two letters.
⟵	**Reread:** Go back and try again.
it	**Cover** part of the word.
sp(it)	**Chunk:** Look for parts you know.
sit pit	Think of a word that looks the same and **rhymes**.
blank ↰	Say **"blank,"** read on and come back.
a e i o u	Try a **different sound** for the vowel.

USE WORDS YOU KNOW

TO READ NEW WORDS

an	**it**	**not**	**see**	**will**
fan	fit	pot	seed	fill
ant	pit	spot	need	bill
ants	spit	spots	feed	kill

TRICKY WORDS

after   away   each   first   help

much   other   pull   their

LEAFCUTTER ANT FACTS

A leafcutter ant colony can contain over 5 million ants.

Leafcutter ants live in tropical areas of South and Central America, Mexico, and in the southern United States.

In the United States, these ants can be found in Texas, Louisiana, Florida, the Carolinas, and even New Jersey.

Leafcutter ants especially like leaves from lemon and orange trees.

Each ant can carry up to 50 times her own body weight.

The mold grown by the ants is rich in nutrients and gives energy to the ants. The mold can't grow without the ants.

A leafcutter ant colony is made up of one or more queens, worker ants, eggs, and baby ants.